Passive Income Toolkit

(2 books in 1)

How to Earn Six-figures Passively with
an Airbnb and Vending Machine
Business

Josh Hall

Table of Contents

Book #1

Airbnb Business Blueprint

A Simple, Step-by-Step System to Turn
Property into a Six-Figure Cash Cow

Introduction

If you have ever thought about running an Airbnb, you have come to the right place. It can seem very confusing and daunting to begin with, but if you have the right guidance, you can definitely do it. There is a reason why Airbnb has skyrocketed in popularity. People are able to connect with others who have properties available to rent for shorter periods of time. This means guests have more flexibility with the types of properties they stay in as well as pricing and experiences. As a host, you have the opportunity to create a business for yourself with whatever property you currently have. Airbnb has so many different options, including renting out single rooms, communal spaces, and entire properties. Whatever property you have on hand and whatever you're looking to invest in, you can definitely find a place for Airbnb rentals.

Throughout this book, we are going to go through a blueprint to help you get started with your Airbnb journey. You will gain information on everything–from discovering why you want to start running an Airbnb, to all of the tips and tricks you need to market and run your property well. This will result in happy customers having great experiences and will also result in you being able to increase your income.

CHAPTER 1

Why Start an Airbnb Business?

Starting an Airbnb business can be one of the greatest things you do for your finances and your own business journey. However, in order to set yourself up right, you need to understand the good and the bad that comes with it. This will allow you to have the entire picture in mind and not have unrealistic expectations. In this chapter, we are going to go through reasons why you should start an Airbnb business as well as the few negative aspects that you might need to consider.

Benefits of Running an Airbnb

There are tons of benefits to running your own Airbnb. It would be pretty much impossible to go through every single one of them, so we are going to go through a few of them that are the most prevalent. These are the ones that people typically mention as their reasons for starting the Airbnb business. It's also the reason they continue on with it because they enjoy the many different aspects of running an Airbnb. If you identify with any of these benefits, you are probably the right type of person to start an Airbnb business.

Time Flexibility

Most of us would agree that having more flexibility in our days is very necessary. We all want to have full control over our time so that we can do what we love as well as take care of our personal tasks. In fact, working from home is such a desired perk in any job, that people will take a salary cut in order to get it. This is not because people enjoy working from their bedrooms, but the fact that working from home gives you some sort of flexibility in your day. When you start an Airbnb business, you have this flexibility for yourself. You are in complete control of your time and can decide when and where you want to do things.

When you sign up to host on the Airbnb platform, you will be given a calendar where you can block out certain days you are not available. If you do not want to handle guests at a specific time, you really don't have to. The date you select will be completely off-limits to any guests and bookings. If you are looking to plan a vacation at any point, you can book those days out so you do not have to be at your Airbnb to take care of the guests. Perhaps you have your family or friends coming into town for a special event– you don't have to ask permission for that time off. Alternatively, you might find that your home is in need of some TLC and you want some time to take care of the issues and repairs. Blocking off these times will allow you the space to take care of your home and ensure that everything has been done right.

When you run your own Airbnb business you do not have to answer to anyone. Even if you don't have a traditional reason for not wanting to open your home to guests, you can do this at your discretion. This really helps you to plan your life around your own schedule instead of working with somebody else's. Time and flexibility are definitely two of the biggest perks that come with running your own Airbnb.

You Would Be In Full Control

Being in full control of your own life and your own business makes you feel powerful and like you have everything together. When you run your own Airbnb business you have full control over every aspect that surrounds it. Running an Airbnb means that you have control over the upkeep and design elements of your house. If you choose to be a more traditional landlord, you lose a lot of the control. This is because your tenants will be able to change things around in your property even if you don't particularly like it. Even though the home still technically belongs to you, practicality states that the home is your tenants. Since they are the ones that are living in it on a daily basis, you will not be able to check how they are taking care of the home or if they are making changes. Airbnb allows you to check in on your home at regular intervals when you are changing guests.

Another aspect of control is control over payments. The Airbnb platform requires the guest to pay before they stay and book at any home on the platform. The owner of the home will get paid and does not have to deal with the stress that many landlords have. Since everything is handled on the platform, there is no need to chase down guests or tenants for their money. You also have full control over how much you charge per night. This means that you can maximize your profits through various different factors. This helps you to increase the amount of money you make per month or per season.

You Get To Meet Different People

This one is definitely for all the extroverts out there. When you run your own Airbnb business, you'll be able to meet lots of different people. People from all over the world will be checking in to your Airbnb. It is basically like bringing the world to your doorstep. I have heard of so many people who have made lifelong friendships through Airbnb. You will find that guests are incredibly friendly, and because you are the expert in the area, they will want to come to you for guidance and assistance throughout their stay. Becoming a great host will allow you to get many return visitors throughout the duration of your Airbnb business.

This actually helps you to expand your knowledge of the world and what is going on in other countries. You get to learn more about what other people are going through and their experiences. Your eyes will be open to things you never would have experienced or knew about before. This is definitely one of the most interesting aspects of running an Airbnb. You will learn tales and stories about multiple people from different ethnicities, backgrounds, socioeconomic statuses, and various other differences. Gaining a new perspective from other people actually expands your insight and allows you to grasp more knowledge. You will find that it allows you to be more empathetic and more understanding of other people. This matters greatly in the world around us as well as in many professional standings. You will find that being exposed to multiple different people helps you to relate to various people you might meet in your everyday life. This might not seem like a traditional benefit from running a business, but it is definitely something that adds richness to your life. Eventually, even the most introverted airbnb host finds out how rewarding it can be to meet various different people from all over the world.

Risks That Come with It

Along with all the positive aspects that come with running your own business, there are also some negatives that you have to consider. It is important to note that many of these things can be managed through time, patience, and strategy. However, in certain cases, you will just have to deal with these negative aspects. Like any business, there will always be risks involved. It will be your job to ensure you're doing your part in order to mitigate the risks. This will give you a better chance of succeeding in your business.

You Might Get Unruly Guests

Unruly guests are definitely going to be a potential risk factor. You will likely not be able to meet your guests until they check in. At this point, it will be too late for you to do anything about it. Collecting a breakage deposit is always a good idea because if your guests were to break something or damage your property, you will have financial compensation for it. Airbnb also has insurance (AirCover) tied to it, so if you do put in a claim for damages, you will likely be fairly compensated. This being said, it is always a huge hassle if you do get guests that do not respect your property and end up damaging it.

Income Is Not Guaranteed

Like with many other businesses, income is typically not guaranteed. Rental properties usually have high seasons and low seasons. This means there are certain times of the year with lots of people looking to book with you and other times where it will be completely quiet. It is up to you to plan for the low seasons so you still have some finances to handle what needs to be done. Planning is definitely key when it comes to this, and there are definitely strategies you can put in place to make your property more attractive in the low seasons.

Clean Up and Upkeep Is Your Responsibility

There are not many people who actually enjoy cleaning up, but at the end of the day, if you own a rental property, it comes with the territory. You will need to make sure that your property is clean and maintained well so that every guest that comes in will have an excellent experience. Guests will be leaving reviews on the platform and getting negative reviews could deter future guests from booking with you. This is why you need to ensure that you are completely consistent with the type of experience you are giving each guest.

Chapter 2

Market Research Stage

Market research is an essential part of starting an Airbnb business. Doing this properly will help you to set yourself up in the right direction. You will have a better chance of attracting the right type of guests and increasing your profit margins. At the end of the day, your Airbnb is a business and you need to be making money from it.

Who Are Your Guests?

When you are trying to do market research you need to understand what your typical guest is going to look like. This is based on various factors. If you already have your property and are looking to rent it out, you will need to understand exactly what type of person would be staying in that area and in that type of home. For example, if you have a one bedroom apartment in the city, a large family is not going to be your target audience. However, singles or couples who are looking to travel and see the city would be drawn to this type of property. If you have a property in the business district of your city, business men and women would also be attracted to that area. You can then target your marketing approach based on the type of people you know will be staying at your property.

Realistically look at the type of property you have as well as the area it is situated in. Try to put yourself in the mindset of somebody who would book that property. You can also go onto Airbnb and find other properties similar to yours in a similar area. Have a look at how they market their properties and to who their target audience is. If you better understand your potential guests and how to market your property towards them, you will be more successful.

Understanding your potential guest is incredibly important because you need to cater to them. Different guests will have different needs. For example, business professionals who are always traveling will be looking for a place that is close to business centers and has access to Wi-Fi. These are the things that are most important to business professionals because they are looking to work. They might also need a designated workspace on the property so that they can take online meetings and have a place to concentrate on their work. This means you can purchase a desk and chairs and create a productive work environment for them. Since you know your target audience, you will be able to understand their needs and ensure that they have the best experience possible. This will result in more repeat guests as well as reviews that show similar guests that your property is the best for their needs.

Assess the Area

If you already have a property, there's probably not much you can do about the area it's situated in. In this case, understanding the type of guest is going to be the most important research you do. On the other hand, if you are looking to purchase a new property for your Airbnb business, you should definitely assess the area before you buy. The area in which your Airbnb is situated is arguably one of the biggest players in whether or not it is going to be successful. Certain locations are simply more lucrative than others. This is for various reasons but there are certain markers to look out for.

If you're looking to invest in a property for short term rentals and Airbnb, you need to look in cities that are quite popular for tourists or business travelers. They should have access to amenities as well as tourist attractions. A city that has a strong economy, great transportation services, nearby shopping centers, and various other amenities will be the best one to invest in.

When you are considering a specific city or area, it is a good idea to understand the high and low seasons. For example, certain cities or states will only be popular in the summer months. Understanding this will allow you to purchase the right property for you. You will also have realistic expectations on the booking potential of the property. Doing some research on the growth of the tourism sector in that city is essential. You would want a town or city that seems to be growing economically. This means you will have a better return on investment. If a specific city looks like it's on the decline, it is definitely not going to be a good investment, as you might end up struggling to advertise the home as well as find it very difficult to sell it if you need to down the line.

These days, it is actually pretty easy to find statistics for Airbnb's in certain cities or areas. All you need to do is type it into your internet search bar and you will get plenty of results that will help you out. Ensure you are cross referencing the data you are receiving, so that you fully understand how each city or state performs. This will help you better decide on which area is going to be the most beneficial to your Airbnb business.

Check Out the Competition

If you want to fully understand how much you could potentially be making in a certain area with a specific property you're looking to invest in, you will need to check out the competition.

Luckily, the Airbnb platform makes this incredibly easy. All you have to do is sign in as a potential guest and research the properties in the area you are in. You will be able to see the types of properties that are available in your area and how much people are charging guests per night. This will allow you to see which properties are the most successful and you can decide on why this is. Perhaps there are certain amenities that are drawing guests in or it could be a specific type of property that is most successful in certain areas.

You will also get a good idea on how to competitively price your Airbnb in regards to the other ones in the area. This will help you to plan out your finances better and ensure that you are not over or under charging for your area. Researching your competitors will also allow you to find out if there are any gaps in the market. If you're able to offer something unique or something that makes your property more noticeable, you will likely attract more guests. It doesn't have to be anything massive; simply offering a small amenity or advantage will definitely attract more people to your property.

Utilizing the reviews on your competitors' properties is also a great way to do some research. You will see why people enjoy staying at certain properties and why they haven't left negative reviews on others. There might be certain aspects of the property that are simply not as desirable as others. You can get some insight into the minds of the guests who stay in a specific area by looking through the reviews. This way, you can set yourself up for success by avoiding any of the common mistakes you find.

If you're feeling a bit stuck when it comes to doing your market research, the good news is that there are plenty of tools that can help you out. These tools can be specific to Airbnb or targeted to general short term rentals. Either way, they can help you to understand your potential guests as well as the area you are looking to invest in. Many of these do come at a fee, but it is an investment towards your business. You'll be able to make better and smarter decisions when you use some of these tools. Here is a list of a few of them that you can check out:

- Airbtics

- AirDNA

- Mashvisor

- AllTheRooms

CHAPTER 3

Operating Plan

Once you have your property and you are ready to prepare your Airbnb for the world, you need to first have an operating plan. Running an Airbnb is not just advertising your property on the Airbnb platform and calling it a day. You need to ensure you have a plan to manage your property. There is a lot that goes into renting an Airbnb, so it is definitely not a passive form of income. If you do want it to be a passive income, then you will need to hire somebody else to take care of the property for you. However, we are going to work under the assumption that you are doing it all on your own. This way, you can create a better business plan for yourself. In most cases, it might be a better idea to start off doing things on your own so you fully understand what goes into running Airbnb. If you do decide to get someone else to help you run your rentals, you can give them proper guidance and you have realistic standards that have been set.

Setting up the Property

The great thing about running an Airbnb is that you can inject your own personality into the property. You can highlight the areas you love about your property so you have a unique space for your guests. Most guests understand that when they're staying in an Airbnb, it is someone's home. That "homey" touch makes it different from staying in a hotel, which can sometimes be too stiff and clinical. Never feel shy about adding a few personal items to the property.

If you are starting with a bare-bones property and you need to fill it with items, you should start with the basics. Think about the rooms that you have in the house and what each room would typically need. For example, the bedroom would need a comfortable bed, extra linen, storage, and a few decor pieces. You can make a list for each room so that when you go shopping, you know exactly what you need to purchase. Keep in mind your target guest and ensure you are filling the space with the things they would need. Not every guest will need every kind of furniture. You don't want to overspend on certain things that are simply unnecessary and will go unused in most cases.

Don't be afraid to move around the furniture and decor pieces in the home. The goal is to make it look as inviting as possible. If it is possible to make the space look bigger by furniture placement, you should consider it. This part of the process is definitely trial and error, and it might take a while for you to discover what works and what doesn't work. You can always change it up as you figure out the better ways to do things.

During the setting up process, it is important to do general maintenance checks as well. You will need to make sure that the plumbing and electrical appliances all work well. It's not going to be a good look on you if your guests are the ones who figure out that things are not working the way they should. You should take some time to hire a professional to check that everything is going to run smoothly. This type of check will need to be done periodically, since general wear and tear will take place naturally.

Cleaning and Turning Over the Property

After every guest, you will need to turn over the property so it's ready for the next one. If you are really busy and have guests back to back, you will only have a few hours to turn over the property. Even if the time in between your guests is quite long, you should still try and clean the property as soon as possible. This is because during the cleaning process, you are also checking to see if there are any damages done to the property or the items in the property. You will need to report this as soon as possible in order to make an insurance claim and notify the guest.

The best thing you could do for the cleaning and turning over process is to create a checklist for yourself. This will help you to streamline everything and ensure that each guest gets the exact same experience. This will also help you to get to every area and ensure that you do not forget anything. Certain areas in the house will need more time and attention than others. Cleaning and restocking certain items should take place at the same time as this will make things go quicker and be more seamless for you.

The first thing you will need to do is to replace all towels and linens in the home. Even if guests have not used a specific area, you never truly know whether it's dirty or not. It is best to stay on the side of caution and clean out everything. Remove towels, bath sheets, bath mats, pillowcases, bedding, and tea towels. You can send them off to be washed and replace them with new ones. Ensure that you also leave a few extras for the guest to use if needed. Then you can move on to the kitchen, since this is likely going to be your biggest cleaning project. You will need to ensure all the dishes have been washed and put away in the correct places. If you have a dishwasher, this will need to be emptied. Have a look at all of the appliances and utensils to ensure they are clean and functioning properly. Fridges, washing machines, and storage cabinets need to be inspected and cleaned out if necessary. You can then wipe down the kitchen surfaces, taps and hardware, and take out the garbage.

Moving onto the bathroom, you will need to clean the toilets and ensure they are spotless. The same goes for the sink, mirror, and shower or bath tub. Have a look to see if anything has been left behind from your previous guests and remove them. You might need to restock things like toilet paper and toothpaste if you do provide this to your guests. Double check the drain holes so you know they are clean and not clogged. Then you can empty the garbage cans and move on to the next room.

The rest of the house will be pretty simple since there aren't many areas to clean. For entertainment areas, living spaces, and the bedrooms, what you need to do is ensure that the floors and furniture are wiped and cleaned. Make sure there isn't anything left lying around and all surfaces that collect dust are dusted well. You can then go ahead and restock any consumable items your guests would need for the day. If you provide things like condiments, salt, and feeding products, have these on hand to provide guests when you are restocking.

During the cleaning process, you are going to be re-staging the house. This means you need to revert to default settings. Sometimes it can be confusing to do this, so one of the best strategies is to set up your house, take pictures, and use this as your guide every time you turnover the property. This way you can ensure that you are keeping the same standard and your guests can expect this standard each time they stay with you. The goal is to make sure that each guest feels like they are being welcomed and taken care of. Making an effort with cleaning can actually help you get amazing reviews. One of the biggest reasons people leave negative reviews is because the Airbnbs they have stayed at have just not been taken care of or cleaned properly. Since this is such an easy fix, make sure that you do not fall into the trap and end up getting bad reviews.

The House Rules

House rules will be the dos and don'ts for your guests when they stay at your property. These are incredibly important so your guests understand what is expected of them and there is no miscommunication between the both of you. It also helps them to evaluate whether your property is right for them. You will have the opportunity to set out your house rules on the Airbnb website. Guests can see it before they book so that they understand what will be expected of them in advance. You can also send them the house rules via email once they have completed their booking and confirmed they will be staying with you.

Simple Is Better

When it comes to writing out any kind of rules, simple is always going to be the best option. If the rules are too long and complicated, then your guests are likely not going to read it and will not stick to the rules. Using simple language is essential, especially if you get international guests. Not every guest staying in your home is going to be a native English speaker. If you use words that are too complicated, you risk losing the attention and understanding of these guests.

Since the rules are posted on the Airbnb platform, it is important to not overdo it. A common mistake is to write too many rules for your guests to follow. The issue with this is it turns off a potential guest from booking with you. At the end of the day, your guests want to have a relaxing stay at your house, and only being able to eat in one corner of the house is probably not what they are looking for.

Your house rules should probably only be around one page. This gives you enough space to write out your most important rules, and limits you so you don't go overboard. Ensure that you send your guests the house rules as well as leave a printed copy somewhere in the house so they can easily access it. A few common house rules are as follows:

- No smoking

- No noise after 10 PM

- Additional guests need to be cleared by the homeowner

- No pets

- Check in and check out times

Safety

Your house rules should also have some safety and security rules in them. This is to ensure that your guests are safe and your property is secured. These house rules can include closing and locking the doors and windows, as well as not lighting any candles, or things that can cause fires. You will likely have a few safety requirements of your own, so be sure to include them in your house rules so your guests are aware of them.

Some Cultural Rules

Every house, host, and country is completely different, so there will be some cultural elements that you might want to add. You can utilize your house rules as a way to educate your guests on specific cultural aspects that you expect from them when they stay in your home. For example, many households require that nobody wears shoes inside the home. If you come from a background like this and you require a guest to do the same, you should add these into the rules. You can even add a little explanation as to why things like this are done.

Emergency Details

Even if you have done your best to ensure that your guests will have a safe stay on your property, emergencies still happen.

Ensure that your guests understand what to do in the case of an emergency. You can highlight where they could find a first aid kit or a fire extinguisher in your home. If there are any natural disasters or the area is prone to certain types of emergencies, notify them and leave a note of how to deal with the situation. You should also leave emergency contact details of the police, fire department, hospital, and your own contact details so that your guests can get in contact with the relevant people in the event of an emergency.

CHAPTER 4

Marketing Plan

Marketing is an essential part of running any kind of business. When it comes to Airbnb, you will be marketing your property on the Airbnb platform. The goal is to stand out from the rest of the properties so that you can get bookings consistently. One thing to note is that even the best marketing will never get you a 100% occupancy rate. This is incredibly unheard of and not something you should be aiming towards. In fact, anything above a 60% occupancy rate is great. This means that of all the listed times available for your property to be booked out, 60% of the time is filled. Having this kind of realistic expectation will allow you to be more successful in your Airbnb endeavors. Applying the tips and tricks we will be talking about in this chapter will aid you in getting high occupancy rates and making the most profit.

Taking Elite Photos

The only way people will know what your Airbnb looks like is through the photos you post on the Airbnb platform. Taking great photographs is one of the best ways to attract people to your property. You will find that the properties that have professional and clear photos are the ones who get the most bookings. There are many things that you can do to help people to live through the photos. You will notice that there are three pictures that show up first on any listing. These will be the most important photos. If you have any unique aspects to your property, you should upload pictures of these aspects to those slots. Perhaps you have an exceptionally large living space, a pool, or an amazing outdoor area. Anything that can grab the potential guests attention so they would be more likely to book with you.

The rest of the photos also have to reflect your property and frame it in the best light. You should have at least one or two photographs for every room or area in the house. People want to actually know what they are paying for when they book through the platform. Try and take your photos at a time of day where light is brightening up the room. Typically, early morning is one of the best times to take photos because the light isn't as harsh but it still brightens up everything. You could also try taking photos at golden hour, which is about an hour before sunset. It is best to use natural light rather than the artificial lights from lamps and indoor lighting. Natural light brings a brightness and a softer feeling to the space. It is also a good idea to shoot your photographs into the corner of a room rather than flat on. This will give the room dimension and make it seem bigger. Try taking a photo on a flat wall and then try aiming a camera into a corner to see the difference. You will quickly notice how much better shooting into a corner makes the photographs look. Try taking many different pictures from various angles so that you can get a better idea of what is working and what isn't.

Another option would be to hire a professional photographer to help you get the best quality photos. This is definitely an investment, but it is worth it if you are able to showcase your house in the best light possible and ensure you get the most bookings. You should never underestimate the power of photographs on the Airbnb platform. If you are unsure of the type of photos you should be taking, you can have a look at other listings and see the difference between the popular ones and the unpopular listings. This will give you a better idea of the photographs that are drawing people in.

SEO and Titles

SEO stands for search engine optimization. When you are able to use SEO you will allow potential guests to find your property a lot easier. When they type in keywords, they will be able to see your property first. The trick is to know what keywords to put into your listing. You can use SEO in the description or the title of your listing.

A great way to see whether or not you were using the right keywords is to do a search test and see where your listing falls on the page. If you are way down at the bottom, you are not using the right keywords in your description or title. If you are quite high up, then you can be sure that you are using the right words. You can look at the listings above yours to see what kind of words they are using that allows their listings to be more visible.

Descriptions

You want your description to pop off the page and attract as many people as possible. Even though your title is incredibly important, your description is what's going to carry on peeking your guests' interest. Your description doesn't have to be very long–as long as it is effective. Whatever you described in your description box needs to reflect in the photos that you have uploaded. Take some time to scroll through your photos and see if you can bring them to life using words.

You should also consider structuring out your description so it's easy for the reader to go through. Using multiple paragraphs with shorter sentences is typically a good idea. You do not need to put every piece of information in your description. All that needs to be there are the most important things. You need to use words that bring life to your property and avoid words that are too generic. If you have a word in mind, you can use a thesaurus to find alternatives that could bring more meaning and visualization to the words on the page. It is also a good idea to speak directly to your target audience and show off the aspects of your property that are going to be beneficial to them. Have a look at a few other properties' descriptions to find out how they've structured them and get some ideas for yourself as well.

Getting Reviews

Getting good reviews is going to be essential when it comes to running an Airbnb. The more positive reviews you have, the more people will want to book for you. There will be a sense of credibility that is tied to your property when there are multiple reviews being left. The first thing you need to do is make sure your customers are all satisfied. If the guests that stay in your property are happy with the service and the experience they've had, they will be more likely to leave a good review. The entire experience will start from the time they have booked until the time they check out. This means you have to communicate with them throughout the process and ensure you are building a good relationship with your guests. This helps them to feel like you really care about them and they will be far more likely to leave a positive review.

If there ever is a problem that pops up, you need to be on the ball. Most people aren't upset by issues that arise, but they will be if they are not being heard. Ensure that you are doing your best to resolve any concerns or issues your guests might be facing. I can almost guarantee you that even if there is some sort of negative experience, your guests are not going to remember if you handled it well enough.

Once your guest checks out, you can send them a check out message that requests some feedback from them. Requesting feedback is a bit more low key than asking for a positive review on the Airbnb platform. It will also help you to get better in the future and know exactly what your guests are looking for. Another great way to prompt your guests to leave you a review is to review them. Airbnb allows both the host and the guest to review each other. Once you send out your review to them, they will only be able to see this review if they leave one for you or they have to wait over two weeks. Out of sheer curiosity, a guest will more likely than not review the host so they would be able to see the review left of them.

Chapter 5

Financial Plan

Working on your finances is incredibly important with any kind of business. You need to have a plan set in place so you do not overspend unnecessarily. Having a financial plan helps to maximize your profit and ensure you are purchasing the right items as well as funneling your money into the correct areas. You'll be able to plan better and understand how much money to raise.

Expenses

Understanding what your expenses are will allow you to create a budget that is realistic. The amount of money you spend on your expenses will be tied directly to how much profit you make. Knowing all the costs will allow you to set a reasonable nightly rate so you are not charging too little and ending up making very little profit. It is important to track all of your expenses throughout the duration of your business. Many of your expenses could change over time and that means you would need to adjust your nightly rate accordingly.

Mortgage

Your biggest expense is going to be your mortgage payment. This will differ depending on the type of property you have. Some people choose to run Airbnb's on the same property they live on, but in a separate room or a smaller property that is on the larger one. Ensure you are only taking out a mortgage that you can afford.

Insurance

It is essential for you to take out a separate insurance for your property, because you don't want to be liable for a large sum of money if guests are injured on the property or if something happens and needs to be replaced or fixed. There are many property insurance plans that target short term rentals. You should get one that covers you in this regard. Traditional property insurance isn't going to cover you if your guest gets injured on the property or if you are sued for some reason. Do your research so you can get the best deal. In many cases property insurance is lumped in with your monthly mortgage payment, which makes it a lot easier to pay.

Utilities

Utilities such as electricity, water, waste removal, gas, and internet will need to come out of your Airbnb revenue. This will likely be the second biggest expense after your mortgage payments. You can expect to pay around 20 to 25% of your monthly costs towards the utilities.

Maintenance and Cleaning

Every property needs to be well-maintained, and this is especially so when you're renting it out to other people. Things like lawn care, plumbing, and electrical appliances will all need to be considered when doing your maintenance. If you are doing maintenance yourself, this will be a lot cheaper. However, it does take away time from you. If you're looking to hire a landscaper or a gardener to take care of your lawn, you need to add this into your budget. The same goes for any plumbing or electrical maintenance.

Cleaning costs can also be considered home maintenance. You can definitely pay somebody to do the cleaning and turn over your home, but you need to ensure they are doing it properly and to your liking. Giving clear instructions to the people who are doing this is essential. It is also important to note that professional cleaning will come at a cost, so you do need to add this to your budget.

Furnishing

All Airbnb's need to be furnished well so your guests have

everything they need when they're staying with you. In most cases, furnishing will be a one time expense unless something breaks and needs to be replaced. It is a good idea to purchase good quality items so they last longer and are more durable. Have a look at what you need in your Airbnb and budget for them in your financial plan.

General Supplies

Your guests would need basic items such as coffee, trashbags, soap, and toilet paper. There are probably many other disposable things that you would like to purchase for your guests and all of these need to be in your budget. Many Airbnb hosts love to create a welcome package for the guests because it adds a personal element to the home. In fact, guests who receive a personalized welcome pack tend to leave better reviews because they feel as though the host has taken the time to really consider them and their needs. You can buy these items in bulk to reduce the amount of money you will be spending on them.

Fees

There are a few different kinds of fees that can be associated with running your own short term rental or Airbnb. When you advertise your property on a short term rental website such as Airbnb, the platform will take fees from the host. All sites will be doing this differently, so you do need to research and find out what the fees will be. Fees could also differ depending on your area. These fees are typically taken out of your nightly rate when somebody books with you. This means you need to ensure you're accounting for the fees when you set the rate on the platform.

Depending on the city or state your Airbnb is in, there might be homeowners association fees and registration fees that need to be paid. Many neighborhoods have a homeowners association that will only allow short term rentals if you are part of the association. This means that there are yearly fees that need to be included in your expenses. Registration fees are when your city decides that every short-term rental needs to register with them. This is becoming more and more common, so be sure you're doing your research so you are not skipping out on this as this could result in penalties.

Taxes

Nobody likes to pay taxes, but unfortunately it is a part of living in a society. There are a few taxes that you will have to consider when you are running your own Airbnb. The truth is, Airbnb has become a major threat to the hotel and rental industry. Because of this, there have been many legalities put in place for Airbnb owners. It is important for you to contact your government offices to find out what taxes you will be liable for.

You will likely need to pay traditional property taxes as well as taxes on the income you are making. The amount of taxes you will be liable for will depend on the city or state you are in.

Chapter 6

Automating and Scaling

As your business grows, it's going to be increasingly difficult for you to handle everything on your own. While you might have been able to do the multiple tasks that come with running an Airbnb when you only had one property, adding two or three properties to your business is going to complicate things. Once you learn how to automate your processes, you will be able to scale your business a lot quicker. Things will become a lot easier for you to handle and you will have a lot more free time to do other things.

Automated Messaging Systems

Guest communication is incredibly important, but it can also be very time consuming. If you have multiple properties and various guests that are constantly checking in and out, it can be so difficult to stay on track with all the communication. Missing out on the communication can leave guests feeling as though you do not care about them, and this can lead to bad reviews. You want to be able to provide your guests with the best experience possible, but you also don't want to be sitting by your computer answering the same questions over and over again.

As a general rule, you should be sending messages to your guests before, during, and after their visit to your Airbnb. You should also be replying to their queries and concerns promptly. One of the best ways you can do this is to have email templates ready to go. If you use an Airbnb automation tool such as "Host Tools", you will have access to templates that will be sent out to your guests at the appropriate times. If you do not want to sign up for tools like this, you can type out generic messages and copy and paste them into the emails as needed. However, this is likely more time consuming than getting a program to do it for you. Here are some of the instances in which you can create message templates:

- Booking confirmations

- Booking inquiries

- Booking requests

- Check in messaging

- A check up message

- Check out message

- Message to leave a review

Check-in and Key Exchanges

Meeting your guests upon check in is doable when you have one or two properties, but as you scale up your business, it's just not going to be feasible. Automation makes it a lot easier for your guests to seamlessly check in and check out of your Airbnb without you needing to be there. Many Airbnb hosts will sign up with a property management company that will do all of this for them. There will be somebody there to help check in and check out the guests, and you have to just pay the fee to the property management company. This is an incredibly convenient way to do things.

Another option is to install smart locks in your Airbnb. When you do this, it is not required for a person to be physically present to handover the keys to the guests. The entries will be keyless and that makes it very secure and convenient. Your guests will receive a unique access code that will expire after they check out. This kind of system is actually way more secure than regular keys because the keys can be copied. If you have a guest that is looking to steal or access the home without your permission, they will not be able to do so when there is a smart lock installed. You do not have to replace locks, replace lost or broken keys, or need to rescue a guest who has accidentally locked themselves inside or outside the home. You'll be able to control everything remotely and it makes the whole process a lot more seamless and less stressful for everybody involved.

If you do not like the idea of the smart lock, there are other options. You can consider getting a lock box or key safe where you place the keys for your guests to pick up. Your guests can then drop off the keys in the same box when it is time for check out. You still do not have to be there while they're checking in and checking out. This is also a cheaper option if you are looking for automation on a budget.

Cleaning Services

Cleaning your Airbnb's is going to take quite a lot of time if you have to do so every time your guests check out. If you hire a professional property management company, they won't be able to handle all of this for you. You should also look into getting a reliable cleaning provider who will come in and clean as needed. It is usually best to go through a company rather than an individual. If an individual cleaner gets sick or is unable to make it to your property when your guests check out, is it going to cause a huge problem for you. When you hire a company, you can rest assured that someone will always be there to clean up and take care of your home. It is definitely a costly option, but you have peace of mind and there will be a higher standard of cleanliness.

Pricing Automation

When you have a short term rental, your pricing strategies need to change all the time. In the high seasons, you can get away with charging more because your property is going to be in more demand. In the low seasons, you can drop your prices so you can still attract people to the home. Pricing strategies can also change from weekdays to weekends. Since weekends tend to be more in demand, you will be able to charge more on these dates. On top of that, you might want to offer some discounts to guests who want to stay for longer periods of time. Having a dynamic pricing strategy is essential to making the most amount of profit through your Airbnb.

You can utilize pricing tools from external sources or use Airbnbs smart pricing data to help you. This will change your pricing based on the data that is provided through researching surrounding properties that offer similar services. You do not have to do anything besides input a few preferences and basic data. After that, it is all up to the software. The program will automatically increase and decrease the prices when necessary.

CHAPTER 7

FAQs and Tips

There is truly a lot of information to take in when you are on the way to becoming an Airbnb host. There are also many tips and tricks that you could implement to help make the process easier and ensure that you and your guests are getting the best experience possible. In this chapter, we are going to go through all of these.

Frequently Asked Questions for Hosts

How do you become a host?

The process to become an Airbnb host is pretty easy. All you need to do is sign up on the Airbnb platform and follow the various prompts. The process is simple to complete and everything you need is going to be on the website. You will need to create an account as well as fill in all the relevant information. Airbnb does not regulate who signs up as a host on the platform, so there won't be somebody coming to check in on your property. Just make sure you create a listing that is attractive, so you can have the best chance of getting bookings.

What is a Super host?

A super host is a regular Airbnb host that has been identified on the platform to provide excellent service. These will have to be experienced hosts who get extraordinary reviews from their guests. Once you reach the super host status, you will be awarded a badge so guests can be notified of this. There will also be a super host filter, and you will likely be able to charge more as one. There are various requirements to be a super host, including: completing 10 trips or three reservations with a total of 100 nights booked, having a 90% response rate, having less than a one percent cancellation rate, and having an overall rating of 4.8 that is maintained consistently.

What is AirCover?

This is simply reimbursement coverage that Airbnb offers to the host. As soon as you sign up as a host, this is automatically applied to you and it is completely free. The host will qualify for up to $1 million in damages and liabilities in the case of issues caused by a guest. With this being said, it is simply not enough to have this type of insurance and you should look into getting your own outside insurance.

What are the cancellation policies like?

There are actually various cancellation policies that you could pick depending on your needs. You can pick a flexible, strict, super strict 30 days, or super strict 60 day policy for your Airbnb. You will have to bear in mind that very strict cancellation policies are a bit of a turn off to many guests and this could lead to getting fewer bookings. You can find out more about the different cancellation policies on the Airbnb website. These can change every now and then, so it is important to stay up-to-date with new information surrounding it.

Tips and Tricks

Create a theme

An Airbnb is supposed to create an experience for the customer. When your guests check in, they should feel like they are on holiday or that the space serves their needs. When you have a theme, everything is cohesive and flows nicely and naturally. It can also help the guests get into the mood of the surrounding area. Your themes can be based on the city or type of location your property is situated in. For example, if you have a beach cottage, you could fill your home with coastal themed furniture and decor pieces. If you have a city apartment, modern and clean finishes might work best.

Give your guests some guidance

As mentioned earlier, giving a guest a welcome package is a great idea. The welcome package can be used as an opportunity to introduce the guests to various places and items they could enjoy in the city, state, or area your property is located in. If you want to get the best reviews, you should do your best to ensure that your guests are having a great time overall. Giving them a list of suggested restaurants, activities, and places to visit is a great way to add a personal touch to your property.

Never oversell your property

One of the biggest mistakes people make when they list properties is they oversell it. They make it seem so amazing and get the guests' expectations too high. The mentality behind this is to attract as many guests as possible. However, it actually has a negative effect on your reviews and the guests' experience. If the guest expects to stay in a five-star resort and is met with a three-star cottage, they are going to be very upset. The ratings will be incredibly low and it will hurt your potential future customers. This is why it's so important to be honest. In fact, it is better to undersell your property slightly, so that you are able to exceed your guests expectations.

You set the expectations that your guests have. You either need to meet them exactly or exceed them. This is the only way you will be able to get the best reviews and ensure that your guests have the best time and experience while they're with you. At the end of the day, even if you have an amazing listing, negative comments and reviews can really bring it down and you will end up losing a lot of credibility.

Consider your neighbors

Even though your neighbors do not pay you any money or are not involved in the Airbnb process, your relationship with them really does matter. Your neighbors could end up complaining and make it very difficult for you to continue with your Airbnb business if they are upset. They could also interrupt your guests' stay for various reasons. This is why you should speak to your neighbors as often as possible and give them whatever relevant information they need. If they are aware that you will be running an Airbnb, they will be a lot more forgiving and can prepare themselves accordingly. You should also ensure you have notified your guests to be mindful of the neighbors so they do not overdo it with noise and disruptions.

Start cheap

When you are first starting out with Airbnb, you aren't going to have any reviews and this means your credibility is quite low. The only thing people have to go on is your listing. A great way to attract more people to your listing is to make your nightly rates cheap. People will be more willing to book at cheaper rates, and you can get a good amount of people to stay at your property. The first few months should not be focused on profit, but rather on getting the word out there and setting yourself up for the future. Once you have built up your business and have a good customer base, as well as some good reviews, you can increase the price to a reasonable rate that makes a profit. You will have reviews that show other guests how amazing the experience was and it will be easier to attract more people to your property.

Conclusion

Running an Airbnb business is one of the most rewarding but also one of the hardest things you're ever going to do. There are tons of new skills that you will need to gain, as well as learning to be flexible and planning properly. As time goes on, you will definitely see what works for you and what doesn't. Even though this is an Airbnb blueprint, every person will run the Airbnb slightly differently. You can learn from other people and their stories, as well as from your own trial and error. You should always be open to learning more about the business so that you can continue to grow with it. There's always new tactics, strategies, and information coming out, so this book is just the starting point. A successful business is one that is continuously growing and changing to play towards the target audience and the market.

You can definitely find success with Airbnb if you are willing to put in the work. The first few months are going to be a lot of hard work because you will be finding your feet. After that, things will start to get a lot easier because you will understand the process and you can start automating. This is when you'll really start to see the fruits of your labor and you will likely enjoy it a lot more. Running an Airbnb helps you to meet so many new people, have great experiences, and increase your income so that you can increase your standard of living.

Book #2

The Vending Machine Business Blueprint

An Easy, Step-by-Step System to Build A Six-Figure Business That Prints Money While You Sleep

Introduction

When you think of passive income, what comes to mind? A rental property? Or perhaps a diversified investment portfolio?

These are what I would call traditional streams of passive income—an investment strategy your parents grew up learning about. However, the world has changed drastically over the past few decades, and there are now modern ways to earn passive income that don't require a trust fund!

A vending machine business is probably not something you dream about. But what if I told you that it is one of the most lucrative passive businesses and that it has low startup costs and low overheads?

Not only does the math add up, the business model is flexible enough to be customized to your niche market. This means that whether you are selling candy or hot pizza, you will always find customers who are looking for on-the-go convenience.

At this point, you are probably thinking, "What's the catch"? The truth is that there is no catch. But like any other business, running a successful vending machine enterprise requires the perfect mix of the right product, price, location, and marketing strategy.

This short blueprint has been created to provide you with the A-Z steps on how to register a business, set up a business plan, buy the right vending machine, manage operational costs, build a reputable brand, and so much more!

If you want to cash in on the $10.2 billion industry and become a vending machine operator, this book is the perfect resource to kickstart your journey. Get ready to learn how to double your income without having to quit your 9-to-5.

Chapter 1

Why the Vending Machine Business?

Chase the vision, not the money, the money will end up following you.
–Tony Hsieh

A Snapshot of the Industry

In the US, the vending machine industry has a market value of $10.2 billion as of 2022 (IBISWorld, 2022). It falls under the Retail Trade Industry and has been ranked 49th in the industry (based on market size).

From the period 2017–2022, the vending machine industry has grown by 0.8% each year on average. However, the increase in demand for on-the-go products and cashless payment systems are just some of the reasons why the industry is expected to see consistent growth.

Growing up, you may remember only being able to buy snacks and beverages from vending machines. But nowadays, this is not the case. While snack and beverage machines continue to lead in the market, new niche products being sold through vending machines are slowly changing consumer purchasing behavior.

To put it simply, pretty much anything that can be bought with money can be sold through a vending machine. This ranges from cigarettes to beauty products, and everything in between. The ability to sell a wide range of products creates an opportunity for operators to generate a significant amount of revenue by strategically positioning their machines in the right location, with the right product.

Potential Earnings

The main objective of starting a business is to generate income. The vending machine business is profitable; however, it is important to remember that not every machine will make money, due to a number of factors such as the type and price of products, as well as where the machine is located, and if there is a big enough demand. Therefore, how much you earn has a lot to do with how your business is structured.

Nevertheless, let's take a look at the numbers!

According to VenTech Media, the average American spends $27 per year on vending machine items and the average purchase amounts to $1.75. A normal snack and beverage vending machine generates just over $75 of revenue per week, which comes to $300 per month (VenTech Media, 2020). Since profit margins on vending machines vary, not every machine will generate $300 monthly. Some may generate much less or significantly more!

The type of products you sell will also affect profitability. The more novel or in-demand your products are, the higher the profit margins you can take home. This is because consumers know that they cannot find those products anywhere else. However, if you are selling soda and snacks that sell cheaper elsewhere, you may not have enough leeway to increase your profit margins.

Startup Costs

Earlier on, I mentioned that running a vending machine business comes with low startup costs and low overheads. This is perhaps one of the most attractive aspects about the business model. Nonetheless, similar to the potential earnings, the total startup costs will vary depending on the type of vending machine you are interested in (more on this in the section below).

In general, the bulk of your investment will go toward

purchasing the vending machine and stock items. The most affordable vending machines go for $300, but the fancier and more high-tech machines can reach upwards of $5,000. If you are working with a small budget, you can get your vending machine business up and running with as little as $2,000.

Please note that startup costs do not include operational costs—the monthly expenses incurred while running your business. Examples of operational costs that you will need to factor include insurance, inventory, maintenance, leasing fee, sales tax, and loan repayments.

Vending Machine Options

When we think of vending machines, we often picture the standard snack and beverage machine. However, this isn't the only type of vending machine available on the market. If you find that your area is overpopulated with snack and beverage machines, you can differentiate your business by opting for a different type of machine. Below is a list of vending machine options you can choose from.

1. Food and Beverage Machines

Machines that stock soda, snacks, and candy are known as food and beverage machines. They remain the most profitable type of machine, accounting for more than 43% of total vending machine revenue globally (Grand View Research, 2019). If you are looking for an option with the least amount of risk, then the standard food and beverage machine is the best pick.

2. Bulk Vending Machines

The most affordable vending machines on the market are the bulk vending machines. These are the miniature machines you find in malls or kids' play areas that are stocked with gumballs, small toys, or stickers. Besides the affordability, these machines require very little upkeep, which means your maintenance costs will be considerably low. The only potential drawback is the potential monthly revenue. The average monthly revenue generated by bulk vending machines is $30. The good news is that the stocked products come with extremely low overheads, so even if you only make $30, you are still walking away with profit.

3. Specialty Vending Machines

If you have a few chunks of change to spend on a vending machine, you may be interested in purchasing a specialty machine. These types of machines are custom-made to stock specific products, or to perform specific functions. Unlike food and beverage machines, it is rare to find a refurbished speciality machine because of how niche they are. Examples of specialty machines include:

- Hot beverages machines

- Electronic gadgets machines

- Luxury products machines

- Alcohol beverages machines

- Beauty and cosmetics machines

- Medication and wellness products machines

- Hot savory meals machines

- Clothing machines

- Laundry products machines

Before settling on this option, find out what items are permitted to be sold in your jurisdiction by contacting local authorities.

4. Franchising Option

The final option is to purchase an existing vending machine franchise with an established customer base and routes. The upside to choosing this option is that you are buying into a business model that has already been proven to work. Your franchisee agreement may even come with free support and training to help you get started. You will also be able to calculate how much revenue you will generate per machine, making it easier to scale your business.

One of the main drawbacks is that you don't have as much

freedom to customize your brand or tweak the business framework. Moreover, depending on your agreement, you may have to pay a portion of your revenue to the franchisor periodically.

There is no right or wrong way to set up your vending machine business. Just make sure that whichever option you choose, you purchase one or two machines with a specific target audience in mind. When you have found the perfect formula for product, price, place, and promotion, you can add a new machine.

Pros and Cons for Starting a Vending Machine Business

With any business comes a number of pros and cons. This is because despite having a solid business model, there will always be factors that you cannot control. Generally speaking, vending machine businesses are attractive for first-time entrepreneurs, as well as those who are looking to build automated businesses. However, with this being said, there are still drawbacks that must be considered. Below are a few pros and cons of starting and running a vending machine business.

Pros of Running a Vending Machine Business

Here are the top reasons why you should be excited about

starting your vending machine business:

1. Low Startup Costs

Starting a business requires startup capital. This initial investment can range from $100 to $100,000. A vending machine can be up and running with just a few thousand dollars to start with. Of course, as time goes on, you will incur operating costs, but these can also be kept to a minimum by, for example, leasing rather than buying a machine, and sourcing products nearby.

2. Low Risk

Since your initial investment is low, you are exposed to less financial risk. You can use the first vending machine to test the market, location, and products. When you have finally found your winning formula, it is safer to invest in a second machine and rinse and repeat the strategy.

3. Flexible Management

Many business owners are drawn to vending machine businesses because they require very little active involvement. This doesn't mean that you can completely abandon your machine, but you will only need to check on it periodically (like once every week), in order to collect money or assess security. If you are currently working a 9-to-5 job, you can set your own business hours and decide on how frequently you replenish stock.

Cons of Running a Vending Machine Business

As attractive as this business framework is, we cannot overlook the drawbacks. Here are some challenges you will need to carefully plan for:

1. Profitability Depends on Scaling the Business

One vending machine can make you break even or pocket a few hundred bucks every month. But, if you are looking to generate thousands of dollars in revenue, you will need to focus on reinvesting into your business and purchasing more machines. Note that if a single machine is making $100 per month, it will take several years before you can purchase a second machine. To accelerate the process, you can seek a business loan and pay it off in manageable monthly installments.

2. Tight Competition for Prime Locations

Vending machine operators know that being situated in the right location is winning half the battle. As a result, operators compete for prime locations, which happen to be in areas with a high population of blue-collar workers. When starting your business, one of the main priorities will be to find a spot that receives sufficient foot traffic, but isn't saturated with vending machines (or at least the type of vending machine you are looking to invest in).

3. Risk of Accumulating Expenses

The profit margins on vending machines are not high. To succeed in the business, you will need to reduce your expenditure as much as possible. Typically, operators budget for monthly expenses, but get a rude awakening when fuel prices increase, when paying exorbitant sales tax, or needing to repair the machine on a regular basis (especially if it is a pre-owned machine).

To avoid the accumulation of expenses, take the time to account for every small and large expense. Try to run your business as lean as possible, so that you have emergency funds to tap into when you are faced with a financial crisis.

Chapter 2

Business Plan to Maximize Success

The best startups generally come from somebody needing to scratch an itch.
–Michael Arrington

Do You Need a Business Plan?

Roughly 543,000 startup businesses are registered each month in the U.S.. Within the first two years, seven out of ten businesses are still operating, but at the five year mark, only five out of ten businesses are active. What's interesting is that 70% of the businesses that make it to the five year mark follow a strategic business plan (Nazar, 2013).

A business plan is more than just a 50 or 100 page document that sits in your office and gathers dust. It is a blueprint that outlines the growth plan for your business. The purpose of the plan is to prepare your business for the journey ahead by setting out the step-by-step processes on how to achieve your goals, increase sales, and build a reputable name for yourself.

If you are planning on seeking funding, most lenders will require you to have a business plan. They will want to see your income projections and if your business model is viable or not, before approving your for the loan. Therefore, not only does a business plan increase confidence in yourself as an owner, it also increases the confidence of your potential investors.

Below are the main components of a business plan that you will need to include when creating your living document. Feel free to customize each section, adding as much detail about your business as possible.

Executive Summary

The executive summary is a one page introduction and overview of your business plan. Many people prefer to write it last since it is made up of the key points mentioned in each section of the plan. The goal of writing the executive summary is to assume that the reader will not have the time to thoroughly go over every page of the document. Therefore, present all of the need-to-know information, such as your business model, direct competitors, target customers, overview of the marketing strategy, and overview of your financial plan.

Company Overview

In this section, you will get the opportunity to introduce your business in more detail. Some of the key elements to include are the industry analysis (snapshot of the market you are entering), the company's legal structure, your vision and mission statement, as well as the company goals and objectives. If you are on top of the game and already have a company brand, this would also be a great place to share more details about it (including logos and other branding elements).

Customer Analysis

The customer analysis focuses on defining your target market and creating various customer profiles. Your goal when writing this section is to think about the people who would be most interested in purchasing items from your vending machine. Your analysis can begin broadly by creating customer segments. For instance, you might come up with two segments: people who work at office buildings and people who work at construction sites. Thereafter, you can break down each segment and think of your customers in terms of their age, gender, income level, and needs and wants.

Competitor Analysis

Since you are not the first vending machine business in your area or the first company to sell food items, you will have both direct and indirect competitors. Direct competitors are those businesses who operate in the same market and sell similar products. In this case, these would be other vending machine businesses. Indirect competitors would be those businesses who are not necessarily competing in the same market, but operate within the wider industry. Examples of indirect competitors for a vending machine business would be traditional restaurants, convenience stores, hot dog stands, grocery stores, and so on.

For each competitor, provide a summary of their business, what they sell, as well as their strengths and weaknesses. When considering their weaknesses, think about it from a customer's perspective. For instance, what needs or wants is the business failing to respond to? The final section of the competitor analysis should include your competitive advantages, in light of what your direct and indirect competitors offer. Here are a few questions to get you thinking about your competitive advantage:

- Are your products niche or superior?

- Will you provide lower prices for goods?

- Will your service be easier or faster?

- Will you provide better customer service?

Marketing Plan

The best way to structure the marketing plan is to focus on

addressing the four P's of marketing: product, price, place, and promotion. Let's briefly look at each "P" and what it entails.

- **Product:** Your product is the vending machine that you will be operating, as well as the products inside the vending machine that you will sell. Mention all of the saleable products and why you have chosen those specific items (i.e. justify why your target customers would purchase those items).

- **Price:** Record the prices for goods and how they compare with your direct competitors' prices. This portion of your marketing plan can be a simple spreadsheet with a list of product prices.

- **Place:** Describe the location of the vending machine and why you have chosen that exact location. Mention any amenities that your location offers that can support your business, such as having plug points, 24/7 security, or being situated close to a cafeteria or food court. You should also justify how your location will bring a steady stream of foot traffic.

- **Promotion:** Create a strategy for attracting customers to your vending machine. Note that there are a variety of ways to promote your services, which can include online advertising or offline signage and branding. You can also look at ways of making your vending machine more appealing, such as keeping it clean, improving machine technology, or placing the machine in a strategic location.

Operations Plan

The first few sections of your business plan explained your goals. The operations plan documents how you will achieve those goals through daily, weekly, or monthly processes. When you finally begin trading, avoid deviating from your operations plan because doing so might cost you more time and money. In general, the operations plan can be divided into two sections: short-term processes and long-term milestones.

The short-term processes include all of the day-to-day tasks that are involved in running your business, such as the sourcing of products, stocking of machines, collecting of money, and keeping the machine safe and clean. The long-term milestones include goals that you hope to achieve in the future, such as purchasing a second or third vending machine, when you expect to hire your first employee, or reaching X amount of dollars in sales by a certain year.

Management Team

Even if you don't have employees working for you yet, it is important to establish a strong management team. At the beginning, you may be the only person on the team. This is normal, but bear in mind that most of the managerial responsibilities will fall on you. Some of the information you can add to this section include your résumé, emphasis on the skills and experience you bring to the business, and an overview of your business title and duties. Feel free to also outsource managerial responsibilities like accounting or managing the operations, while growing your business and getting it to a point where you can hire an in-house team.

Financial Plan

The financial plan is usually the last section of your business plan (unless you are going to include an appendix). It typically includes a 5-year financial snapshot of your business, broken down into monthly or quarterly statements for the first year, then annual statements for the remaining years. The type of financial statements you can include are income statements (also known as a profit and loss statement), balance sheet statements, and cash flow statements.

Compiling a business plan can take anywhere between one month to one year. What tends to speed up the process is having all of your research ready. It is also helpful to carefully analyze your plans, processes, and systems before writing them down on your business plan. This will ensure minimal issues when you apply them later on. Weigh their strengths and weaknesses and compare them to what your competitors are doing or the latest trends in the market.

CHAPTER 3

Buying the Right Machine

Behold the turtle, he makes progress only when he sticks his neck out.

–Bruce Levin

Factors to Consider When Buying a Vending Machine

Having the money to buy a vending machine is one thing, knowing which kind of vending machine to buy and what to look out for is another. It is important to remember that no vending machine is the same. Some are new, others are refurbished, and many of them vary in design and technology. Therefore, when selecting a vending machine, think about what your particular business needs are. Below are a few factors to consider when purchasing a vending machine.

1. Type of Vending Machine

The type of vending you choose will be informed by the

products you wish to sell. If you are going to sell beverages, you will need to buy a beverage vending machine. Refer back to Chapter 1 and have a read over the vending machine options available to you.

2. Location

Another key factor is location. Certain types of vending machines work best in certain locations. For example, hot beverage machines do well in office buildings because of the number of people who buy hot coffee or tea in the mornings or late afternoons, whereas a bulk vending machine serving pieces of candy may do well in children's play areas. When picking a location, consider the demographics of customers in that area and what those customers are likely to purchase from your machine.

3. Easy to Use

One of the biggest advantages for buying items from a vending machine is the convenience factor; customers who are on-the-go can spend less than five minutes buying food and drinks. When purchasing a vending machine, think about how quick and easy it is to transact. The more complex the system, the less likely customers will return. In general, if a 10 year old finds the machine easy to use, then most customers won't have much trouble using it either.

4. Safety

When purchasing a vending machine, consider the safety of your customers too. There shouldn't be any injuries incurred during the buying process. As the vending machine operator, you will be held liable for any accidents involving your vending machines. Therefore, complete your safety checks, include warning labels, and make sure customers understand how to use the machine (you can add step-by-step guidelines on how to purchase items).

5. Size

The location and amount of space you have to place your vending machine will determine its size. It is recommended to measure the space first before deciding on a particular size. Mini machines are suitable for smaller spaces and larger machines work best when you don't have any space restrictions.

The Cost of a Vending Machine

The cost of a vending machine can range from $100 to upwards of $5,000. There are many factors that determine the cost, such as the type of vending machine, whether it is new or refurbished, and how modern the technology is. Buying a refurbished machine may be more affordable, however you should take into consideration the kinds of features customers are looking for.

For example, in these modern times, customers prefer cashless "pay-and-go" systems that make buying easier. Some may even prefer specialty vending machines that offer products one would typically find in a drug or grocery store. Ideally, you will want to buy a vending machine that offers you modern features, at the lowest cost. To find these gems, be prepared to do extensive research and negotiations.

Where to Buy a Vending Machine

Finding a vending machine has never been easier! All it takes is an online search. The difficulty comes in narrowing down your search and finding the most reliable machine suppliers–locally or internationally. The truth is that there is no shortage of vending machine suppliers, but not all machines are built with the same quality and standard. Never settle on the first supplier you come across; do your research and compare what you can get from different businesses.

To help you begin the search, here are three types of sellers you will find online:

1. Manufacturers/Wholesalers

These types of sellers have the widest range of vending

machines (both modern and traditional) available on the market. Not only do they sell vending machines, many of them also offer additional services like repairs and training.

2. Secondary Market Sellers

Also known as specialty online retailers, these sellers have an online marketplace that gives you access to different vending machine brands and models. Some websites may even include helpful resources for entrepreneurs to successfully run their businesses.

3. Consumer-to-Consumer Platforms

Online marketplaces such as eBay or Craigslist host thousands of listings for vending machines. In most cases, the listings come from vending machine owners who are looking to sell their pre-owned machines at affordable prices. The risk of buying a machine through these types of platforms is the issue of quality. Since the machine is not new, nor was it bought straight from a manufacturer, you are not guaranteed that it is of the highest standard.

When deciding on a seller, make sure to look through the customer reviews online. Avoid sellers with less than three star ratings, as well as those who have poor customer service. Ideally, you need to look for sellers who are reliable, offer seamless delivery, and are available for ongoing support and machine maintenance.

CHAPTER 4

Stocking Your Vending Machine

Every day that we spent not improving our products was a wasted day.
–Joel Spolsky

Popular Items to Stock in Your Vending Machine

A crucial factor that determines your business's profitability is the types of products you sell. You might have the latest high-tech vending machine, but if you get the products wrong, your machine won't make a lot of money and it will be a bad investment. When choosing products, avoid thinking about what you would purchase, but instead consider what the majority of your customers would purchase. At the end of the day, they are the ones who will visit your machine on a daily or weekly basis, so stocking their favorite items will help you keep customers coming back.

Different customer segments will have unique vending machine preferences, but in general, here are some of the products consumers find most attractive for vending machines:

- Snacks (Snickers bars, Clif bars, pop tarts, Sun chips, granola bars, nuts and seeds, pretzels, dried fruit, popcorn, etc.)

- Drinks (Bottled water, energy drinks, vitamin water, cold coffee, soda, iced tea, etc.)

- Mini meals (Soups, noodles, rice dishes, pasta dishes, breakfast bowls, etc.)

As much as soda and snacks sell really well, more and more consumers are seeking healthier food alternatives. If your customers fit under the demographic of people who live healthy and active lifestyles, consider adding a few healthy options inside your vending machine to accommodate them.

Best Places to Buy Vending Machine Products

To keep your expenses to a minimum, it is crucial to source your products from the right suppliers. Similar to the process of sourcing a vending machine, you will need to conduct an online search. You will notice that there isn't a shortage of product suppliers in your area or abroad. However, once again, each supplier might offer different perks, customer service, and product quality. Avoid choosing the first supplier that you come across. Take your time to compare different suppliers, so that you can find one that offers value for money.

Here are the types of product suppliers you are likely to come across while doing your research:

1. Wholesalers

Wholesalers offer the widest selection of products at the lowest prices on the market. Some may give you the option of buying in bulk or small quantities, while others may enforce a minimum order quantity. Due to their large-scale operation, wholesalers are able to ship products to you from anywhere in the world. Many of them also have great return policies, like being able to replace products within 24 to 48 hours.

2. Cash and Carry Suppliers

These companies are often associated with a major wholesaler. They operate similar to a grocery store and allow business owners to buy products in bulk at competitive prices. Even though you might end up paying more for goods than a wholesaler, you won't have a minimum order quantity. One of the drawbacks however, is that many cash and carry suppliers don't offer shipping, which means you will need to drive to the store to pick up your products (this becomes an issue the farther away you live from a store).

3. Brokers of Specialty Products

There are also agents who run private distribution businesses that specialize in sourcing and selling specialty products. Most of the time, these products cannot be found in major retail stores due to how niche they are. If you are operating a specialty vending machine, partnering with an agent can help you identify niche product manufacturers to work with. Initially, the cost of working with an agent is expensive, but once you have established good relationships with manufacturers, you can cut out the middleman ("agent").

4. Membership Clubs

Membership clubs are offered by companies like Costco, Sam's Club, and BJ's. Membership is open to the general public; however, it is typically attractive to businesses looking to purchase wholesale products for discounted rates. Membership clubs operate similar to cash and carry suppliers, except you are able to buy goods at wholesale prices. Membership fees will vary for each club, but you can expect to pay about $50 annually.

When sourcing products, you can use more than one type of supplier. For example, you can source bulk items like bottled water directly from wholesalers, and seasonal items from membership clubs. The aim is to keep the costs down to a minimum, while sourcing quality products and making sure you have a wide range of products available for customers to choose from.

CHAPTER 5

Location Is Key

You just have to pay attention to what people need and what has not been done.
–Russell Simmons

Factors to Consider When Looking for the Right Location

Another factor that affects the profitability of your vending machine business is the location. Your goal should be to get as close as possible to your target customers. Of course, this isn't always easy since the competition in the market is already tight. You are likely to find a number of vending machines already situated in the hot spots where your customers spend a large portion of their time. Nevertheless, this shouldn't discourage you. You can still find prime locations by closely examining the following factors.

1. Look for High Foot Traffic

It is important to place your vending machine where you are most likely to get a lot of foot traffic. This is why you need to have a good understanding of where your customers are located. To have consistent sales, you should target repeat customers; those who purchase items on a daily or weekly basis. When considering location, find a spot where customers walk past on a recurring basis, such as a hotel lobby or cafeteria.

2. Study Your Competition

In such a competitive environment, you need to study and monitor your competitors to identify the hot spots. Situating your machine near competitors can be advantageous because it shows that the particular area experiences high foot traffic. With that said, too much competition is never a good thing. As a general rule of thumb, if there are more than 10 vending machines within a specific radius, look for a spot farther out.

3. Ask for Permission

The most stressful part about finding the right location is getting permission from local authorities or the property owner. Before signing any contract, make sure that you agree with the terms and conditions, such as the lease agreement, commissions payable, and legal restrictions imposed in the area. Moreover, different laws and rules apply to different vending machines, and each state may have their own specific clauses. Contact your local chamber of commerce to find out more about vending machine regulations in your area.

10 Popular Vending Machine Locations

Searching for prime locations doesn't need to be a hassle. Below is a summary of the best locations for vending machines. Take the time to research and evaluate each location to see whether it would be suitable for your business, in your specific area.

1. Apartment complexes and condos

2. Office buildings

3. Schools and universities

4. Hospitals

5. Nursing homes/care facilities

6. Car dealerships

7. Construction sites

8. Hotel and motels

9. Gyms

10.   Retail stores, food courts, and shopping centers

There are vending machine locator services available for business owners. These services are run by agents who scout the city looking for the best locations for your vending machine. They take various factors into consideration, such as your monthly leasing budget, the target customers, and the types of products you sell.

One of the drawbacks with using this type of service is the large fees which are charged upfront. This makes you vulnerable to scammers who take your money but have no skill or experience in finding the right vending machine locations. Another drawback is that once they have found a list of locations, they cannot guarantee that your products will sell. Therefore, there is still a considerable amount of risk that you open yourself up to when working with a locator service.

Finding the best location on your own takes more time, but reduces a lot of risk. You will need to do most of the legwork by yourself, such as researching locations, determining the potential profits for each location, contacting owners and property managers, and following up with each lead. The benefit though is that you have more information available to decide on the best location, and you will have already established a relationship with your future landlord.

CHAPTER 6

Managing Your Operations

Anything that is measured and watched, improves.
–Bob Parsons

Day-to-Day Operations of a Vending Machine Business

Even though a vending machine business is considered a type of passive investment, there are minor daily tasks you will need to perform to keep your machines running smoothly. The more machines you own, the more tasks you will need to do! Fortunately, you can hire an assistant or driver to perform many of these tasks on your behalf. Below is a snapshot of the activities you will need to perform on a day-to-day basis:

- Collect products from your wholesaler or nearby storage facility.

- Check to see which items need to be restocked in your machines and plan your routes (unless you have a remote-controlled machine, you may need to physically check stock levels).

- Pack your products in your delivery vehicle and head over to each machine. Refill your machines.

- Assess any wear and tear, or signs of vandalism.

Depending on how many customers purchase from your vending machine on a daily basis, you may be able to get away with refilling your machine once per week. Moreover, having an intelligent machine can save you a lot of time on reporting stock levels, calculating how much money you have earned, and other statistical and accounting information.

Software to Streamline Your Operations

If you are a serial entrepreneur or someone working at a 9-to-5 job, you won't have the luxury of time to spend on actively running your vending machine business. Fortunately, there is software on the market that can take care of many administration and process tasks on your behalf. Below is a list of popular vending machine software available on the market.

1. Quickbooks

Keep track of your business transactions and financial records with Quickbooks. It is a comprehensive accounting software that takes care of most bookkeeping tasks. Some of these tasks include calculating income and expenses, drawing monthly reports, and preparing your taxes.

2. MyVendTrack

MyVendTrack is a mobile-friendly vending route software that handles tasks like managing inventory, planning routes, calculating taxes on each machine, and doing cash readings.

3. Telemetry

Track inventory from the comfort of your home or office with Telemetry. The software tells you when your vending machine is running low on stock so you can head over and refill it.

4. VendSoft

A great all-in-one tool to use for your business is VendSoft. It has been designed to take care of management tasks and streamline the operations of your business. The software focuses on three goals: optimizing inventory, streamlining operations, and increasing business profits.

5. Seaga Smartware 360

Seaga is a vending machine manufacturer that has designed software to manage information on a machine level. For instance, the software is able to read the temperature of the machine, input calorie information for products, set product pricing, and many more features. The only drawback is that the software can only work with Seaga manufactured vending machines.

Handling the Maintenance Needs

Vending machine repair and maintenance costs can be expensive. As an operator, your main objective will be to reduce the likelihood of machine breakdowns and ensure maximum uptime. The simplest way to avoid repairs is to purchase a new machine from a reputable brand. The more reliable the brand, the better. If you are going to purchase a refurbished machine, go for the newest model that you can get. It is also important to make sure that sourcing parts for your particular model is relatively easy and inexpensive.

There are also specific ways to take care of your machine that can reduce the likelihood of maintenance work. Below are a few tips on how to look after your machine to avoid serious problems.

- When cleaning your machine, use food-grade detergent, warm water, and a soft cloth. You might need to wipe down the glass, buttons, and dollar bill validator once a week, but the machine itself only needs a clean two to three times per year.

- Position your vending machine about four inches away from the wall to ensure there is sufficient space for air to flow at the back of the machine. Overheating can lead to wear and tear, which means more frequent repair work.

- Make sure that the ground the machine is placed on is level. Uneven surfaces may lead to breakages and damage.

- If your vending machine is situated outdoors, make sure that it is not placed in direct sunlight. Too much exposure to the sun can lead to overheating and machine malfunctions.

- Double check the electrical needs of your vending machine. Look at the manual to see how much voltage it can take and make sure that the right amount of power flows. This can reduce wear and tear, as well as electrical issues or injuries.

Responding to a breakdown as soon as possible can reduce downtime and save you a lot of money. You can leave a sticker on your machine with your contact details so that customers can inform you of machine issues and other complaints immediately.

CHAPTER 7

Scaling vs. Growing Your Business

You don't learn to walk by following rules. You learn by doing and falling over.
–Richard Branson

Signs to Either Scale or Grow Your Business

It is every entrepreneur's dream to reach a point where they are required to expand their business. It basically means that their business has enough opportunity to make more profits! However, it is important to clarify the difference between scaling and growing a business, as these terms are typically used interchangeably.

When you grow a business, you invest more capital to expand operations, hire more people, or purchase new technologies. This is different from scaling a business, which in contrast doesn't require you to invest significantly more capital, but instead it requires you to find ways to streamline processes and be more resourceful, so you can minimize overheads and maximize revenue.

Here are common signs to look out for when it is time to scale your business:

- **You have a reliable stream of customers.** Not only does your machine attract new customers, it also draws returning customers. This has given you enough financial stability and confidence that your business can see an increase in demand in the future.

- **Your revenue has reached a plateau.** You may be breaking even or making a profit each month; however, you have noticed that there isn't a lot of cash left over after paying expenses.

- **There is a lot of room for your team to improve.** You have been fortunate enough to recruit a dynamic team, but you have not yet maximized their potential. By making a few adjustments to the workflow, you believe that you can get a lot more out of your team.

When it is time to grow your business, you will experience different kinds of problems. Here are three signs that you can look out for:

- **You have been turning down lucrative business opportunities.** Due to not having the capacity to take on more work, you have turned down a number of opportunities, such as missing out on a prime location to place an additional machine.

- **You have surpassed all of your goals.** Achieving all of your goals is a clear indication that it is time to grow your business. Failing to do so could lead to stagnancy.

- **Proven business model and reliable infrastructure. If** you have successfully established a vending machine in the right location, with the right products, and have a strong cash flow and repeat sales, then you have enough expertise and experience to rinse and repeat the concept in another location.

Of course, these signs are not a guarantee that your profitability will continue to increase; however, they are good indicators that your business is healthy enough to expand without incurring too much risk.

5 Ways to Scale Your Vending Machine Business

One of the advantages of scaling your business is that you don't have to pay an exorbitant amount of money to maximize your revenue. All that is required is a few tweaks to your systems and processes to create more income-generating opportunities. Below are five ways to scale your vending machine business.

1. Position Your Machine In Locations With High Foot Traffic

It is perfectly okay to relocate your machine once you have found a better position. When a location with high foot traffic becomes available, such as an office building, airport, or shopping mall, organize for your machine to be situated there instead. A few things that you may need to consider is your current lease agreement and the new lease that you will need to sign at the new location.

2. Switch Up or Diversify Your Products

One of the reasons why your revenue reaches a plateau is due to a decrease in demand for your products. Customers, especially those who make repeat purchases, get bored when choosing from the same selection of goods, over and over again. Switch up your catalog of products or offer niche products that take your customers by surprise! This can also be a great way to test new products that have entered the market to see how well your customers respond to them.

3. Keep Your Machine In Good Condition

An inexpensive way of scaling your business is to properly maintain your machine. This means making sure it is clean, well-stocked, and everything is functioning as it should. If you have money to spare, consider branding your machine with wrapping and signage to make it stand out from the rest of the machines within close proximity.

4. Promote Your Business on Marketing Channels

You can reach more potential customers by advertising your vending machine business on social media. Think of it like marketing any other retail business. Filter your search to look for members of your target audience within close range to your vending machine. For example, you would target people working within a business district or those who frequently visit a specific shopping mall. Take the time to build your social media presence by interacting with users, running competitions, offering coupons, and linking users to your website or blog.

5. Upgrade Your Machine

The final strategy is probably the most expensive out of them all. However, think about this way: Would you rather save costs by upgrading your machine, or spend an exorbitant amount of money buying an additional machine, paying rent for a new location, and increasing your total overheads? If you are sold on the idea of upgrading your machine, then consider buying machines with features that entice customers, such as a cashless payment system, touch screen ordering system, voice-activated customer service, and so on. The upgrade will increase revenue and keep your customer satisfaction high!

It is never advised to wait too long before you make the decision to either scale or grow your business. Ideally, you don't want to reach the point where your revenue plateaus before adjusting your processes. Bear in mind that it is not always necessary to invest more capital in your business to achieve maximum revenue. Sometimes, all it takes is finding new ways to promote your business or improving the condition of your existing machine.

Chapter 8

Laws and Regulations

Diligence is the mother of good luck.
–Benjamin Franklin

Getting the Right Paperwork for Your Business

Before you start operating your vending machine, you will need to check off a few legal requirements to keep your business in good standing. Below are some of the legal steps you will need to take to obtain the necessary licenses and permits.

Register a Legal Business Entity

The first step is to register your business. This process shouldn't take a lot of time, as long as you know what type of business structure you would like to go for. You have the option to choose between an LLC, partnership, sole proprietorship, and corporation. Each structure has its advantages and drawbacks; however, most business owners in the U.S. opt for an LLC, since it limits the owners' liability in case of lawsuits, bankruptcy, and other legal issues.

Register for Taxes

Once you have formed your company, you will need to register for federal and state taxes. The first step to do this is to apply for an EIN. The types of taxes you pay will depend on the business structure you have chosen. You can learn more about small business taxes by contacting the local IRS offices.

Open a Business Bank Account

Another way to limit your personal liability is to open a dedicated business bank account. Opening a separate bank account will also give you an opportunity to build your business credit profile, so you can gain access to business loans and other credit products.

Obtain the Necessary Permits and Licenses

Vending machine businesses who are caught operating without the necessary permits and licenses incur hefty fines, or in extreme cases, have their operations shut down. The first permit you will need to obtain is a vending machine permit. This is a requirement enforced by each state in the U.S., and must be met before the machine is situated at its location. Contact your state authorities to find out how to obtain a vending machine permit.

In addition to the permit, you will need to obtain a business license. Some of the information that is required on the business license application include:

- Federal EIN

- Sales tax number

- Beverage license (if you will be selling beverages)

- Food service license (if applicable)

- Detailed process plan about how you will install the vending machine

Once your application has been received, you will be contacted to schedule a site visit/inspection. The inspector will determine if the machine is situated in the right place and meets the local regulations.

If you are going to be selling food, you may also need to apply for a license with the local health department. They will also send an inspector to check whether or not you meet the health and hygiene regulations.

Apply for Business Insurance

Business insurance is not considered mandatory, but not getting insurance would be taking a costly risk. You want to ensure that your business profits are secure in the event of losses, injuries, or lawsuits. There are different types of insurance products to choose from, depending on your budget. The simplest and most affordable type of insurance is widely known as comprehensive business insurance.

CHAPTER 9

Establishing Your Team and Optimizing Customer Service

Your most unhappy customers are your greatest source of learning.
–Bill Gates

Signs to Hire Your First Employee

With the perks of semi-automated machines and vending machine software, you will be able to handle the day-to-day business tasks for the first couple of years. However, as the business grows, and you begin to manage more than one machine, managing the business alone will become strenuous. Below are some of the signs that you are ready to hire your first employee.

1. You Have Enough Work

An obvious sign of hiring someone is when you have business

tasks that are too much for one person to manage. This may not be the case if you are operating a single machine, but as soon as the number of machines increases, so will the workload.

2. You Have Enough Time to Train the Employee

Hiring an employee, especially the first one to work in your company, requires a lot of commitment. You want to ensure that the employee understands your company vision and their list of duties. Most of the time, they will be representing you when you are not available to meet with suppliers and customers. Thus, it is important that you train them according to the way you would like them to perform work tasks.

3. You Can Afford To

One of the barriers to hiring someone is your company's financial stability. Some of the costs associated with recruiting an employee include:

- Recruitment costs, such as advertising, and conducting interviews and background checks.

- Employee wages, including benefits like worker's compensation.

- Unemployment and payroll taxes.

- Equipment and materials needed to perform their duties,

like stationary, laptops, WiFi, telephone contract, etc.

Your company's cash flow will determine whether hiring someone is possible or not. Avoid judging your cash flow on a good month; evaluate how much money you have consistently coming in over a 12-month period. You should be able to tell if you can afford to hire someone on a contractual, freelance, part-time, or full-time basis.

Tips on Selecting the Right Employee for Your Business

As a general rule of thumb, never hire the first person you interview. Why? Because you have no one to compare them to. Unfortunately, small businesses don't have the luxury of recruiting the wrong person and starting from scratch again. The process is simply too costly to repeat unnecessarily. Therefore, when starting your search, be mindful of what you are looking for and compare candidates to find the one who best meets your criteria. Below are a few tips about finding the right employee for your business.

1. Be Clear About Your Company Vision

When you are clear about where your business is heading, and the goals you need to reach in order to achieve your vision, then finding an employee who has the capacity to assist you becomes much easier. You are able to qualify or disqualify applicants based on the type of skills and expertise you are looking for. You can also decide whether to hire someone on a part-time or full-time basis.

2. Don't Overlook Culture Fit

As important as skills are, being able to maintain a good work relationship is also vital. The type of people you recruit to your company must match the company's culture. In other words, they should share the same values as the company and be willing to adopt the company's work style. During the interview stage, you will be able to pick up on the candidate's personality and work preferences. You can also take note of how they conduct themselves and the type of work background they come from.

3. Don't Make the Decision Based on Gut Instinct

The job candidate might be charming and have an impressive résumé, but don't let their presence cloud your judgment. Before making the final decision of whether to hire the candidate or not, do a background check to make sure they are who they present themselves to be. Your background check might include calling their previous employers to verify work details, checking to see if they have a criminal record, and doing a quick Google search of their name and surname to see what comes up. If you are still not certain about the candidate, you can get a second opinion from a trusted colleague by conducting a second interview.

How to Keep Your Customers Happy and Coming Back!

The benefit of hiring an employee is that you now have someone who can interact with customers, both in person and online. You can train your employees on how to respond to customers and find new and interesting ways to keep them happy. For instance, when a customer has a complaint about your products or wants their money back, your response time should be impeccable. Below are a few strategies that you can practice (or train an employee) to increase customer satisfaction.

1. Keep the Machine Working

There is a common stereotype depicted in movies of products getting stuck inside vending machines or vending machines being out of service. Unfortunately, this stereotype has some truth to it! Far too often, customers experience problems related to purchasing goods from vending machines. You can improve customer satisfaction by simply making sure that your machine is always working. The less problems are associated with your machine, the more likely customers will recommend it to others and return to buy again.

2. Be Quick to Respond to Complaints

The shorter your response time to customers, the more likely they are to trust doing business with you. A great way to reduce response time is to apply a label on your vending machine with your business contact information written clearly. You can also include social media account handles to offer customers different communication channels.

3. Be Consistent with Refilling Your Machine

Repeat customers will likely become familiar with your refilling patterns. It is important to restock products on the same day, at the same time, to accommodate customers' buying behaviors. For example, you might have some customers who expect a certain snack in the morning or late afternoon on their commute to work or home. They would be frustrated to not find their favorite product available. For added transparency, add a label explaining which day of the week your vending machine is refilled.

4. Be Considerate of Your Customers' Preferences

You will be able to tell which products your customers love and which ones they don't seem interested in based on your inventory levels. Whenever you are purchasing new stock, be mindful of what your customers prefer to buy. There is no point in buying more products that hardly get touched. Take note of the brands, product sizes, and most in-demand items that your customers love. Every now and again, surprise them with a new product and test to see how they respond!

5. Maintain Good Relations with the Point of Contact

Even when you have an employee, there will always be someone based on the premises who is the point of contact with your customers, meaning they are likely to receive direct complaints when the machine isn't working or when customers want to find out more information. This person could be the security guard at the office building, hotel staff who hang around at the lobby, or anyone else who isn't on your payroll, but essentially represents your business. Find ways to reward this person by giving them free products or showing gratitude for the way in which they represent your business and motivate customers to return.

The co-founder of LinkedIn, Reid Hoffman said "No matter how brilliant your mind or strategy, if you're playing a solo game, you'll always lose out to a team" (Dropdesk, 2020). While it is possible—and often necessary—for startup entrepreneurs to start their businesses playing the solo game, eventually they will need to put together a team to help the business grow and keep customers happy. Finding the right people to join your company isn't as simple as vetting for skills. They also need to share the same values and passion that keep the momentum of your business going.

CHAPTER 10

Frequently Asked Questions (FAQs)

I knew that if I failed I wouldn't regret that, but I knew the one thing I might regret is not trying.

–Jeff Bezos

FAQs About Starting and Running a Vending Machine Business

1. Can you make a lot of money from a vending machine business?

Certainly. Vending machine businesses are profitable. However, similar to any kind of business, it takes more than a business model to make a company succeed. Some of the main factors that determine profitability for this type of business are choosing the right machine, positioning it in the right location (preferably one with a lot of foot traffic), and stocking your machine with products that customers love.

2. Do I have to pay tax on my vending machine?

Yes. Vending machine operators will be taxed on the revenue generated from each machine. The amount of sales tax payable will vary for each state. Keep an organized record of your finances to make filing taxes effortlessly.

3. What sizes do average vending machines come in?

There is no such thing as an average vending machine since they come in different options and can be customized for each business. However, if we are looking at a typical beverage machine, the average dimensions are 80" H x 40" W x 35" D. Be sure to check the size of the area before purchasing your machine.

4. How long does the process to install a vending machine take?

The time it takes to install a vending machine depends on the supplier. However, on average it can take 15–20 days for your machine to be installed from the day you make a deposit or full payment, to the day it arrives on the premises.

5. Can vending machines be rented out?

Of course, there are businesses across the country who lease vending machines, or offer a rent-to-buy agreement. This may be an affordable option if you don't have a lot of startup capital but are not prepared to downgrade on the type and model of your vending machine.

6. What type of electrical outlet do I need to run my machine?

Most vending machines use 115 volts at 10–12 amps to operate. This means that you need a standard three-prong outlet to power your machine.

7. What can I do if my vending machine is vandalized?

It can be upsetting to find your vending machine vandalized. Not only does this affect your business by causing downtime, but it can also set you back financially. The best way to protect your business against vandalism is to install cameras on the machine or nearby, ensure that the location has 24/7 security, and most of all—get yourself covered with insurance.

8. How many product slots does an average vending machine have?

While vending machines vary in how they are designed, a standard snack and beverage machine has about 8–10 slots to insert products. Note that the sizes of the slots can be different for each machine.

9. How much commission will I need to pay the property owner where my machine is situated?

Not every property will charge a commission for placing your machine on their premises. For some owners, they regard your vending machine as free marketing to lure customers into their property. However, you may get owners who want a commission from your profits. This could range between 0–20% of net profit. The commission and other terms of trade can be negotiated, and will appear on your signed contract.

10. If I want to purchase an existing vending machine business, how do I get access to that information?

The best place to search for vending machine business for sale is online. Look for online marketplaces that specifically deal with selling businesses. As part of your background check and screening of potential companies, contact the following state resources:

- Federal Trade Commission (1-877-382-4357)

- National Fraud Information (1-800-876-7060)

- Small Business Association (1-800-U-ASK-SBA)

- Better Business Bureau (www.bbb.org)

Conclusion

Starting and running a vending machine is not a walk in the park, but neither is starting any kind of business. Nevertheless, when compared to other startups, particularly those in the food and retail industry, a vending machine business is what I would call startup-friendly.

If you have never previously run a business before, or perhaps have too much on your plate to actively manage a business, then this low-maintenance and semi-automated business is for you!

Most of the time, money, and effort you will need to invest will be upfront. But once you have the legal paperwork sorted, location locked, and vending machine purchased, the only major work you will need to do is restock your machine with products and count all of the money you will be making!

The best time to have started a vending machine business was yesterday because, truth be told, the competition in this market is incredibly tight! However, today is also a good day to get started on setting up your business.

This blueprint has been designed to give you the framework for running a successful vending machine business. You will need to do your part and research which strategies will work for you and your specific business model. Don't be afraid to do the work—it will eventually pay off!

If you have found this blueprint valuable, kindly leave a review.

Thank You

Before you leave, I'd just like to say, thank you so much for purchasing my book.

I spent many days and nights working on this book so I could finally put this in your hands.

So, before you leave, I'd like to ask you a small favor.

Would you please consider posting a review on the platform? Your reviews are one of the best ways to support indie authors like me, and every review count.

Your feedback will allow me to continue writing books just like this one, so let me know if you enjoyed it and why. I read every review and I would love to hear from you. Simply visit the link below to leave a review.